HEAVENLY DAYS

Cartoons by

Carol Meiling

published by About Comics, Camarillo, California

Heavenly Days

Originally published by Abbey Books, 1957
About Comics edition published Septemb, 2018

ISBN-13: 978-1-936404-90-2

Customized editions available

Send all queries to *questions@aboutcomics.com*

"Tell me when we have enough for a luscious apple pie."

"Anybody here like turtle soup?"

"Not an angel in sight!"

"I will not jeopardize my standing in heaven for the
fire department."

"You know all about animals Mr. Buck, how can we get a
vicious little mouse out of our room without hurting it?"

"Let's be practical, hamburger has as much protein as filet-mignon and besides it's only sixty cents."

"A modern Saint Francis."

"Of course I know how to fix a flat, but not without a jack."

"Can we borrow your automobile jack . . . and will you come show us how to work it?"

"Who's up?"

"All good things come from heaven . . . just what our team needed!"

"Pssst! Hey Joey, c'mon in, the coast is clear!"

"Oh come on Sister, it's cheaper to buy a play-ground whistle."

*"Oh my! Five teaspoonfuls! The manager is staring
right at you."*

"I guess we'll have to start learning Chinese to
meet competition."

"Okay, let's make it 'even-Stephen', now I'll give you a book
of MY tickets . . . and it will cost you only one dollar."

"It feels lots better, let's come back some other time."

"I'm giving arithmetic tests today."

"Of all things . . . a wallet . . . how nice Jimmy!"

"I'm sure I had two of them in here this mornng."

"It could be the piano needs a tuning, Sister."

"Our talkative little novice is practising some
self imposed silence."

"... and now we will pray for the one amongst us who uses scented soap."

" . . . *and at the sound of the bell she will arise with alacrity.*"

"Crew-cut or duck-tail?"

"Quid est?"

Mother always said I had long spring-curls when I went to kindergarten."

"We have 'souls' and 'soles' to tend to, haven't we,
Reverend Mother?"

"Out with it? Who broke the jardinier in the visitor's parlor?"

"No more coffee for Father Dunn after his morning Mass,
he's too rough on sugar."

"Mr. Gates doesn't give easily but let me do the talking,
I know all his stock phrases."

'Let's get a REAL sun-tan."

"Pssst! Hear the latest? There's going to be a strike
at the local soap works."

"We're from the Mother House, she's the cook *and*
I'm the laundress."

"I know I don't get much melody out of this thing,
but I just love rhythm."

Each year he donates the same pair of homing pigeons."

"... and we'll put your name on a big bronze tablet right inside the main entrance for all posterity to see ... please Mr. Murdock?"

"That's Joe Sylvester, he used to plunk on rubber-bands in class."

"We don't need an exterminator, the mice leave here of their own accord desperately despondent and destitute."

"MY! Look at those tissue thin slices, we must have the most
accurate slicing machine in the world."

"*A-HEM! . . . and don't forget to save me some.*"

"Pssst! Pull over, there's a juke-box going across the street."

"Things get mighty dull down here during Lent."

"Okay Mr. Riley, it's Saint Patrick's Day, but this year make sure you get back in time and condition to ring the Angelus."

"Have you heard of the penalties imposed upon those who argue
with the Reverend Superior Umpire?"

"It's not fair . . . someone should put that new Sister from
Guatemala hep to where she should stand and how
she should swing."

"Couldn't expect much for sixty dollars Reverend Mother."

"It's potage-aux-legumes-Richelieu, but don't let that fool you,
it only means vegetable soup in French."

"Fresh from the Monastery garden, Reverend Mother."

"Never mind modern improvisations on old themes and just
let's stick to straight church stuff."

"Not so much wax in the halls Mr. Finnerty, it's a source of temptation to our novices."

". . . and whose turn was it to water the window-boxes this week?

"Very nice of you, but we have plenty bones of our own down in the kitchen."

"It's a gift for Reverend Mother . . . but not an
alarm clock, PLEASE!

"Sure, I know it would be cheaper to buy another ball of yarn, but where would I get the moola from?"

"You better look for the trouble inside Mr. Pemberton, because last year we found a family of mice nested in there."

". . . and furthermore, your son's arithmetic home work was much better before you started helping him out with it."

"They're at it again!"

"Oh my! The check comes to four dollars, we shouldn't have had that strawberry short-cake for dessert."

"You got any influence with Santa Claus, Sister?"

"If she could do the figure eight in Roman numbers, I would consider her REAL good."

"I told you I didn't need a companion on this trip."

". . . now and at the hour of our death . . .

The Daily Nun

A different nun cartoon in your feed every day!
Nun cartoon caption contests!
Follow **@dailynun1** on Twitter or Instagram!
More information at **DailyNun.com**

www.ingramcontent.com/pod-product-compliance
Lightning Source LLC
Chambersburg PA
CBHW071848020426
42331CB00007B/1907